ALFRED's
SACRED PERFORMER
COLLECTIONS

MW00805188

Sunday Mornin
Special Services Companion

34 Selections for Weddings, Funerals, and Other Services

Arranged by Victor Labenske

The sixth volume in the *Sunday Morning* series, this book contains music for times of celebration, times of sorrow, and times of sacrament. Over a third of these arrangements are for weddings. Since wedding music often needs to be adaptable in length, I have arranged several of these pieces with options for shorter and longer versions. I have also included the most commonly used wedding processionals and recessionals in both traditional and contemporary styles. Another large portion of this collection is devoted to music for memorial services and funerals. While most of these pieces are highly reflective, in recognition of the deep emotions felt during this difficult time, a few are celebratory in nature. The remaining selections represent music that is meaningful for communion and baptism services. My prayer is that these arrangements will be helpful to you and your congregation as you minister to people during these significant times of life.

Victor Labenske

Produced by Alfred Music
All rights reserved.   Printed in U.S.A.
ISBN-10: 1-4706-1045-0
ISBN-13: 978-1-4706-1045-6

Cover Photos
Statue of an angel with flowers isolated on white with clipping path: © shutterstock.com / Kamira •
Blue eyed baby girl in a white dress: © shutterstock.com / FamVeld

CONTENTS BY SERVICE

(Approx. Performance Time – 2:15)

Ave Maria

Franz Schubert
Arr. Victor Labenske

Slowly (♩. = 58)

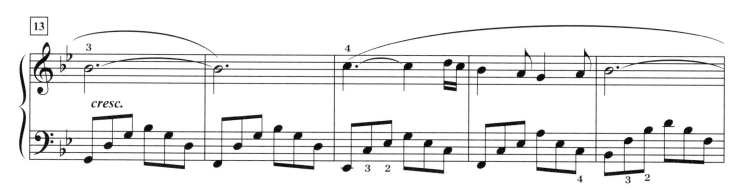

4

(Approx. Performance Time – 2:45)

ABIDE WITH ME

William H. Monk

Arr. Victor Labenske

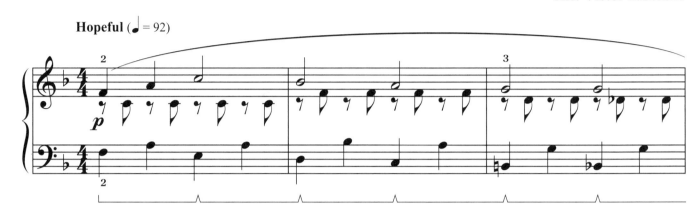

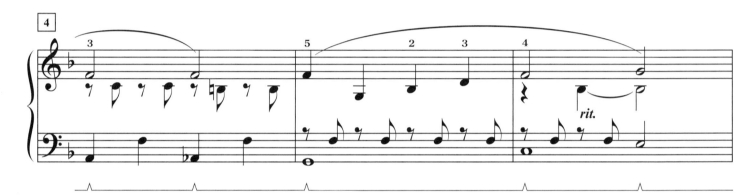

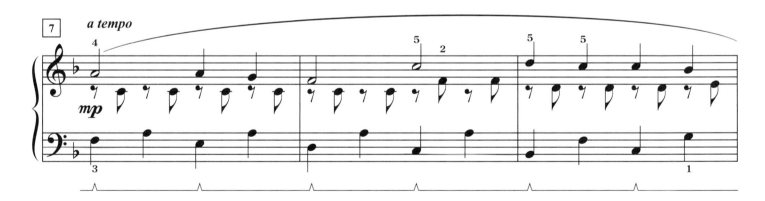

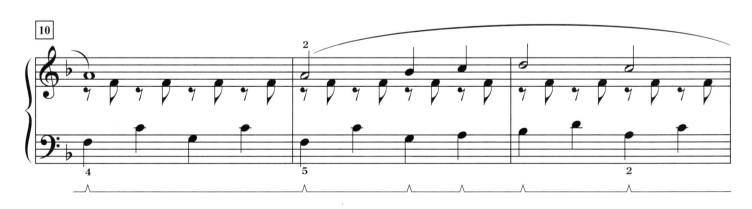

(Approx. Performance Time – 3:00)

Ave Maria

Charles Gounod and J. S. Bach
Arr. Victor Labenske

(Approx. Performance Time – 3:00)

Beneath the Cross of Jesus

Frederick C. Maker
Arr. Victor Labenske

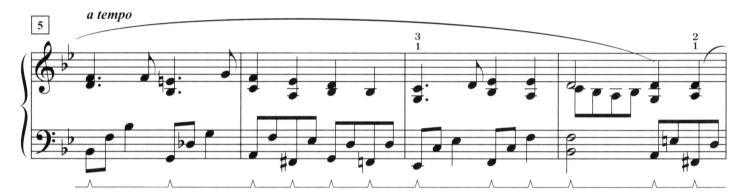

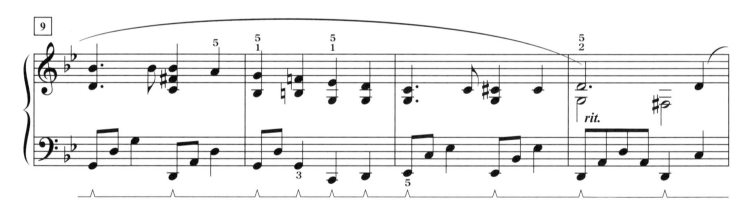

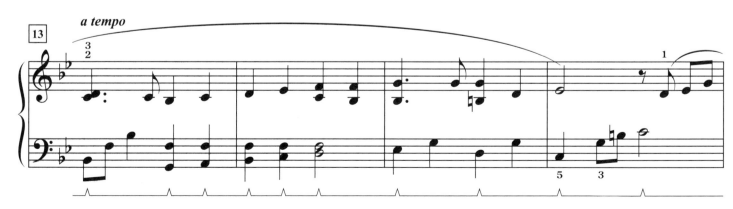

15

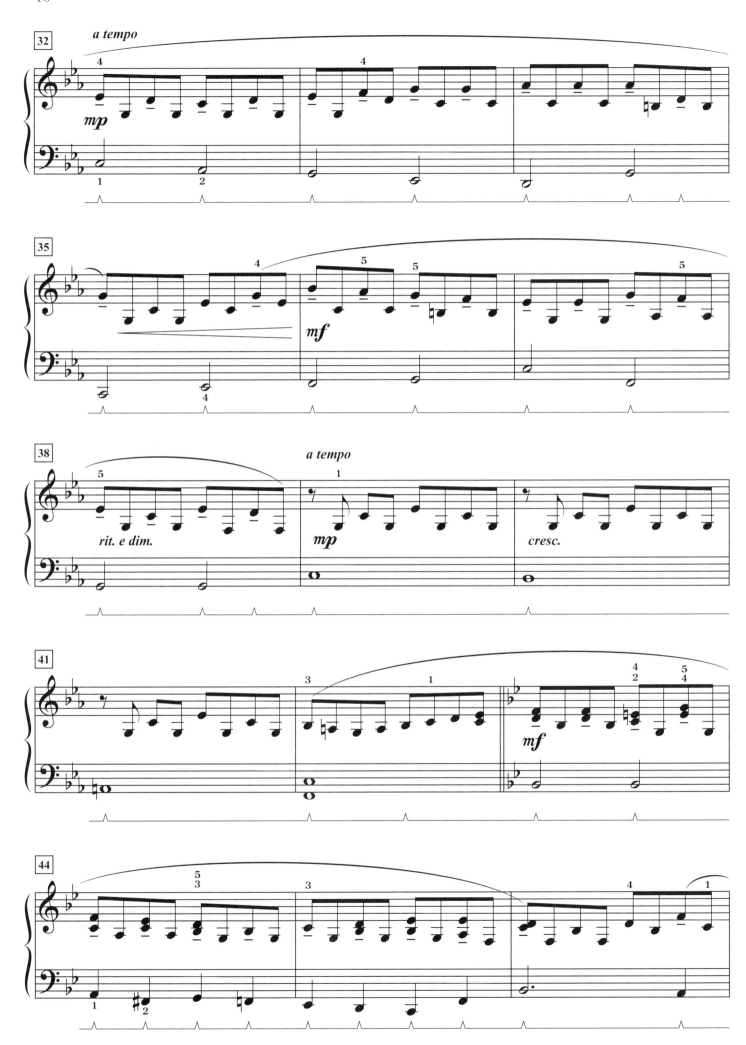

(Approx. Performance Time – 1:45)

If Thou Art Near (Bist du bei mir)

J. S. Bach
Arr. Victor Labenske

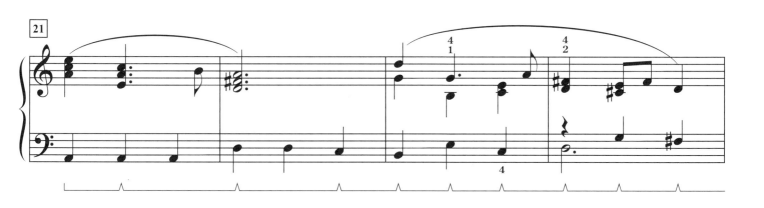

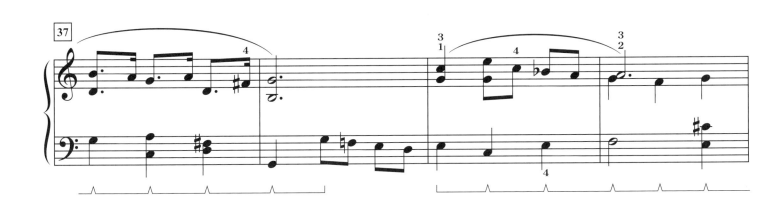

(Approx. Performance Time – 3:15)

BRIDAL CHORUS FROM *LOHENGRIN*
(TRADITIONAL VERSION)

Richard Wagner
Arr. Victor Labenske

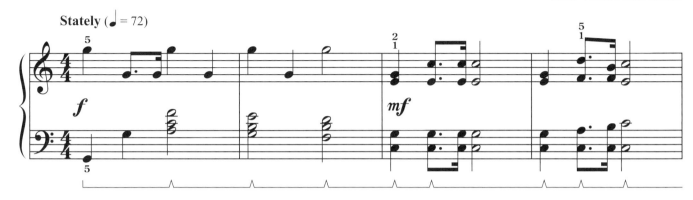

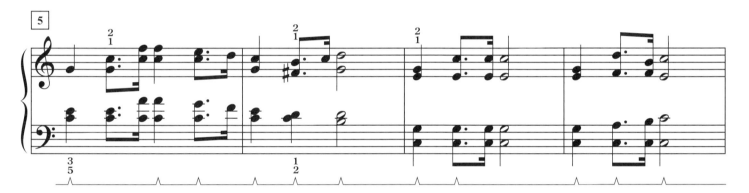

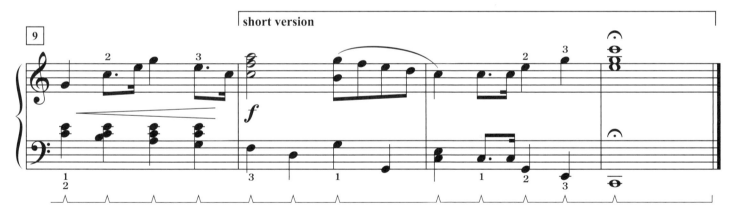

(Approx. Performance Time – 4:00)

BRIDAL CHORUS FROM *LOHENGRIN*
(CONTEMPORARY VERSION)

Richard Wagner
Arr. Victor Labenske

(Approx. Performance Time – 2:45)

Day by Day

Oscar Ahnfelt
Arr. Victor Labenske

(Approx. Performance Time – 4:00)

Canon in D

Johann Pachelbel
Arr. Victor Labenske

Note: The pianist may shorten the piece by jumping from one double bar to another.

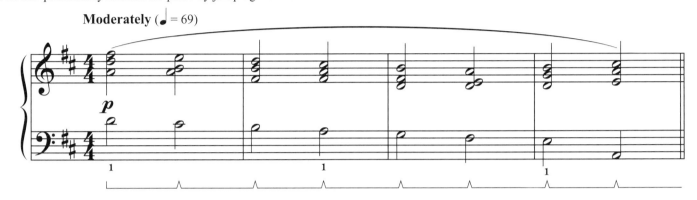

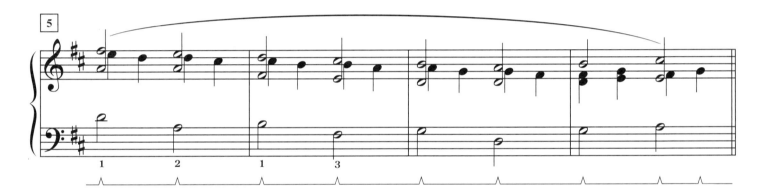

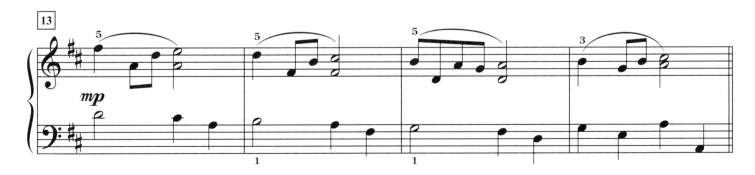

(Approx. Performance Time – 2:30)

Down By the Riverside

Spiritual
Arr. Victor Labenske

(Approx. Performance Time – 1:45)

GIVE ME JESUS

Spiritual
Arr. Victor Labenske

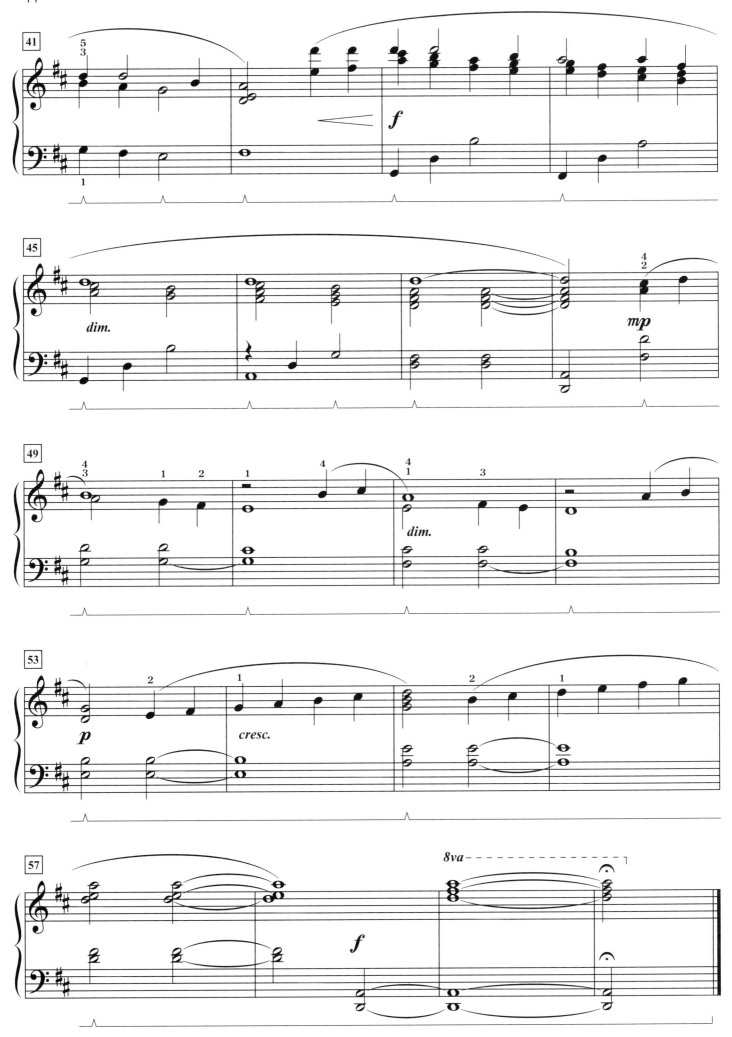

(Approx. Performance Time – 2:45)

HE HIDETH MY SOUL

William J. Kirkpatrick
Arr. Victor Labenske

With devotion (♩ = 112)

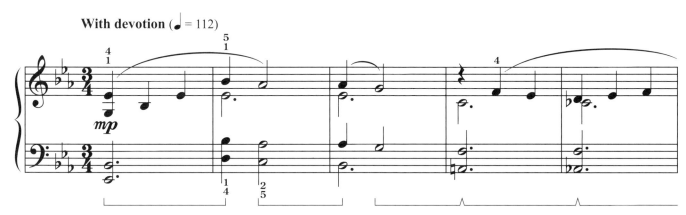

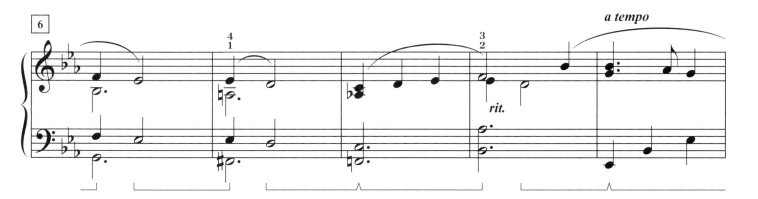

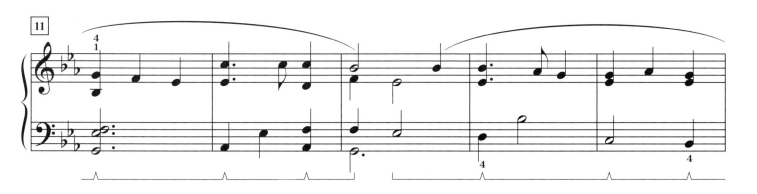

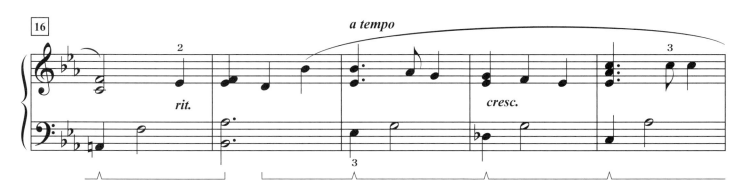

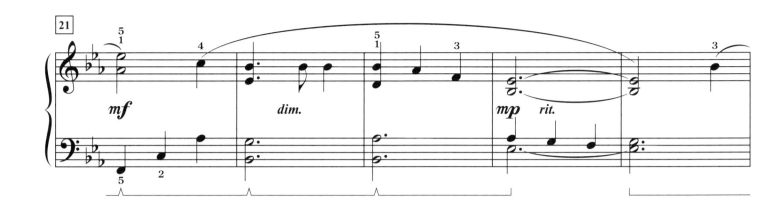

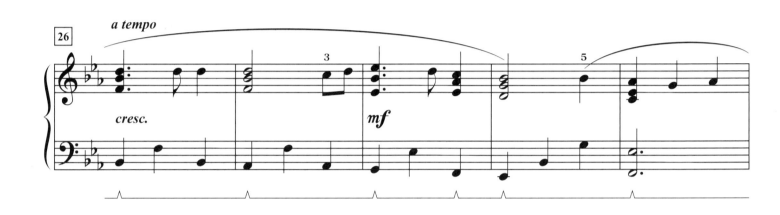

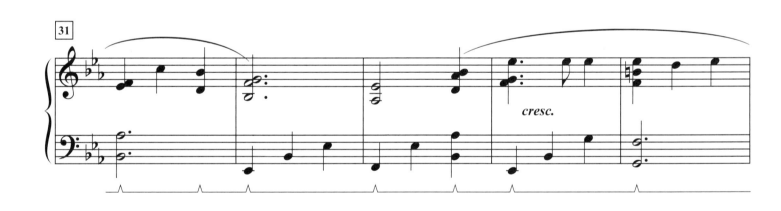

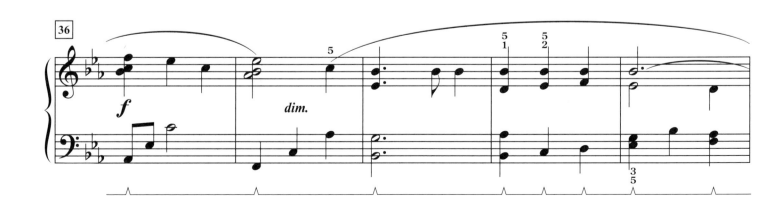

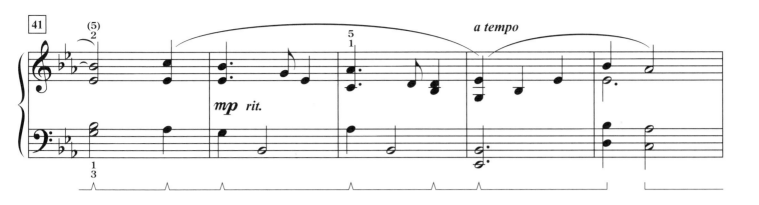

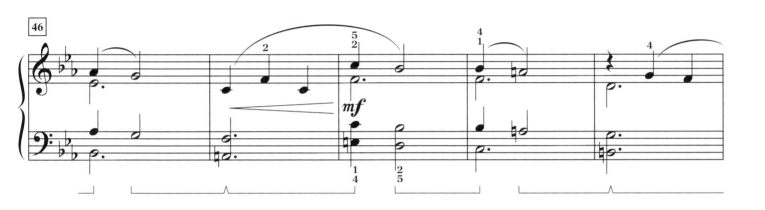

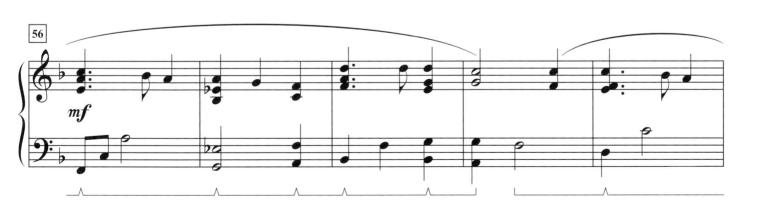

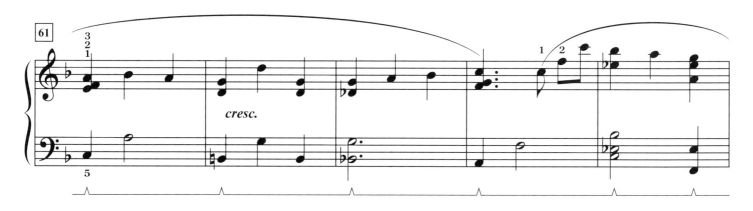

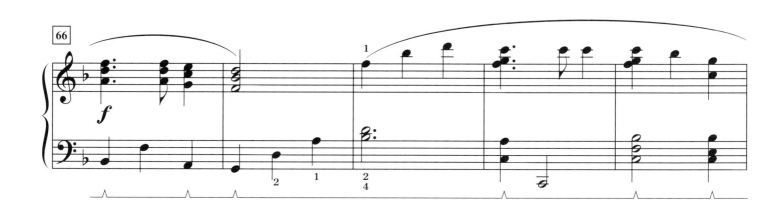

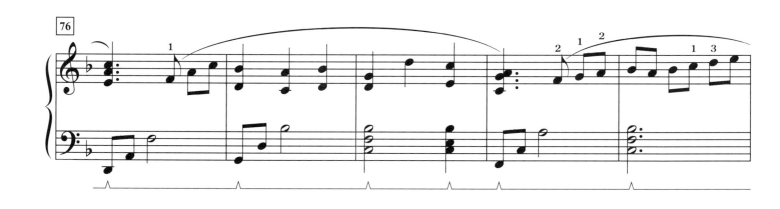

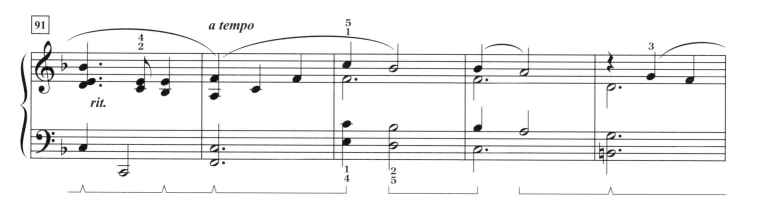

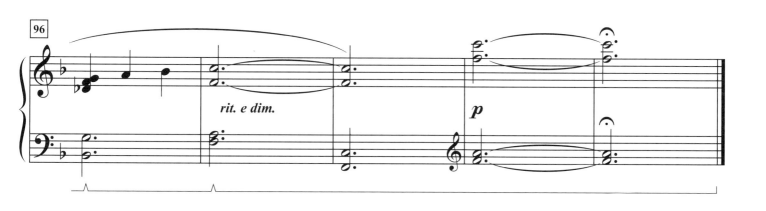

(Approx. Performance Time – 5:15)

Home Across the River Medley
(Steal Away and Deep River)

Spiritual
Arr. Victor Labenske

With longing (♩ = 84)

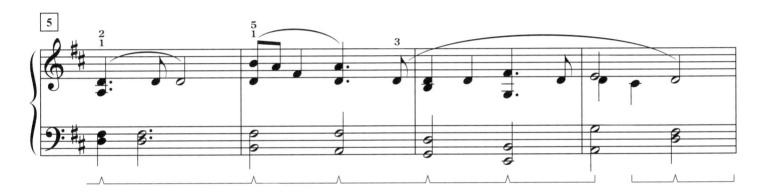

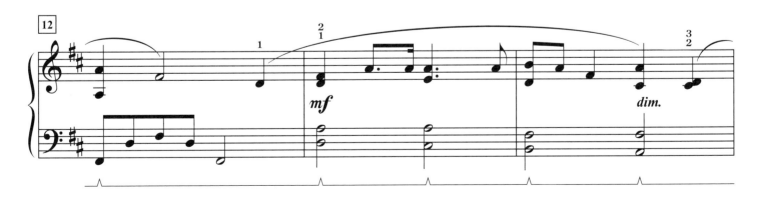

53

(Approx. Performance Time – 2:30)

In the Cross of Christ I Glory

Ithamar Conkey
Arr. Victor Labenske

57

(Approx. Performance Time – 2:30)

In the Garden

C. Austin Miles
Arr. Victor Labenske

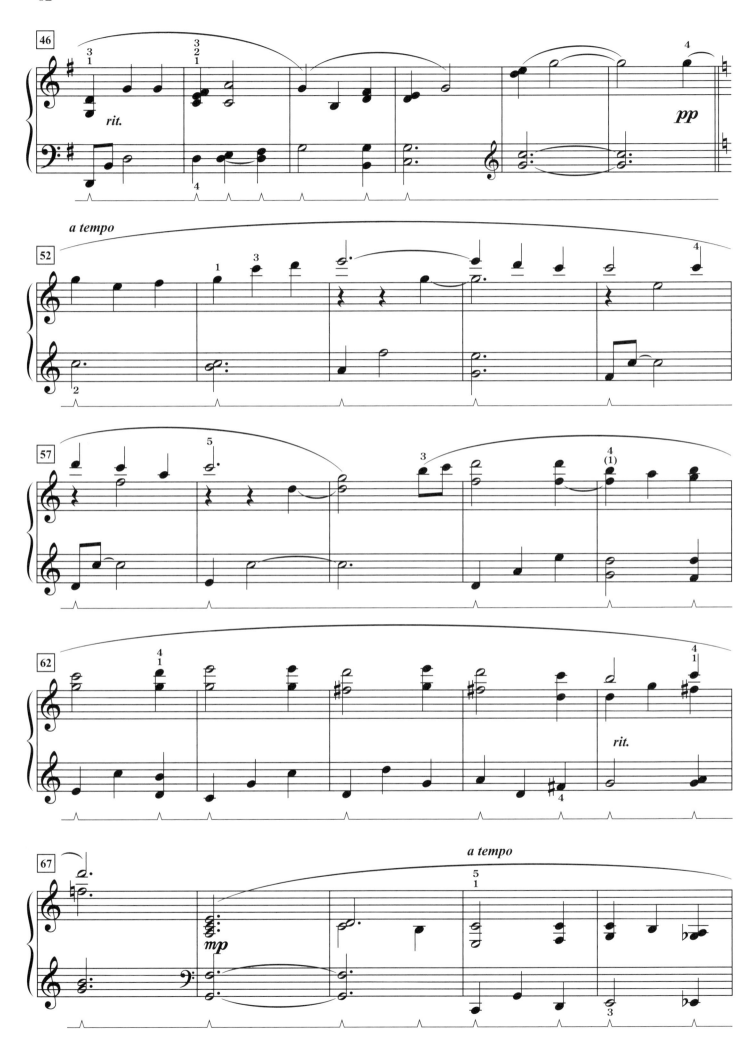

(Approx. Performance Time – 3:15)

Jesus, I My Cross Have Taken

Leavitt's *The Christian Lyre*
Attr. to Wolfgang A. Mozart
Arr. Victor Labenske

65

(Approx. Performance Time – 3:15)

JESU, JOY OF MAN'S DESIRING

J. S. Bach

Arr. Victor Labenske

Note: At any double bar, the pianist may jump to the Coda for a shorter version.

71

(Approx. Performance Time – 2:15)

Largo from Xerxes

G. F. Handel
Arr. Victor Labenske

(Approx. Performance Time – 2:00)

Let's Go Down to the River to Pray

Spiritual
Arr. Victor Labenske

In quiet reflection (♩ = 66)

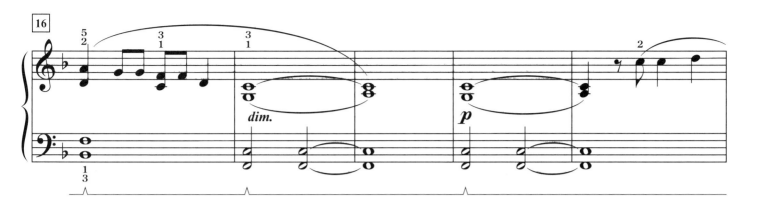

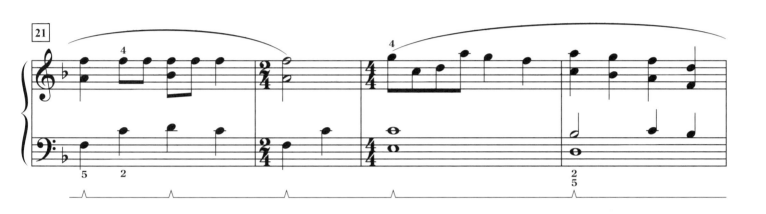

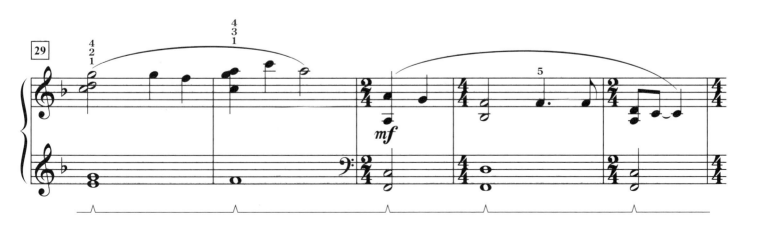

78

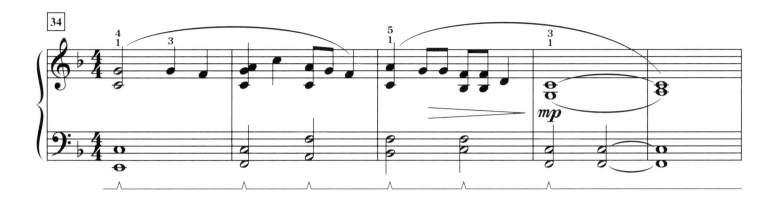

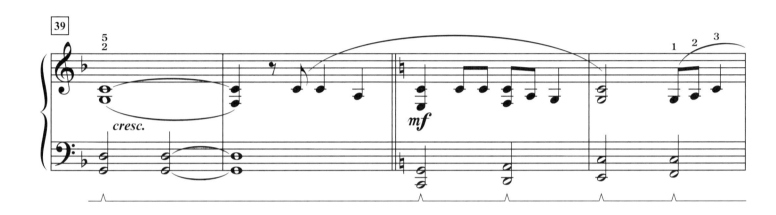

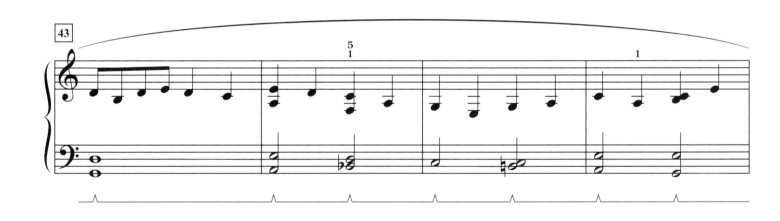

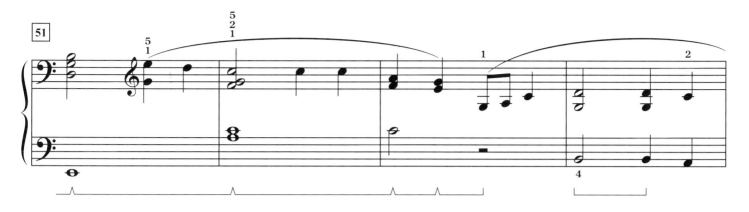

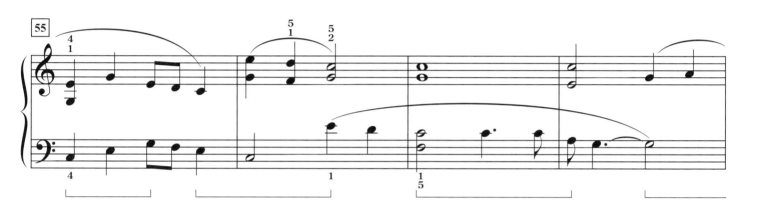

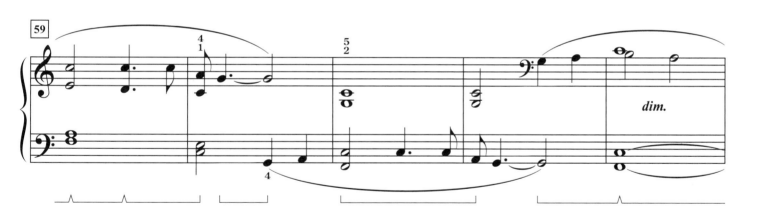

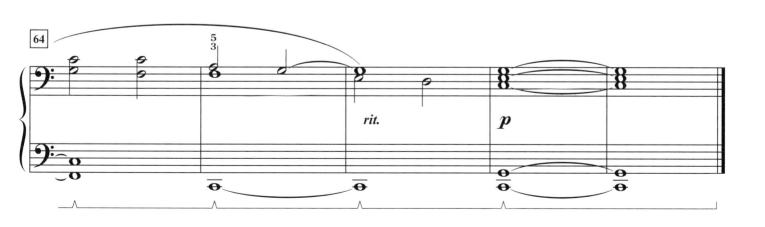

(Approx. Performance Time – 1:45)

Let Us Break Bread Together

Spiritual
Arr. Victor Labenske

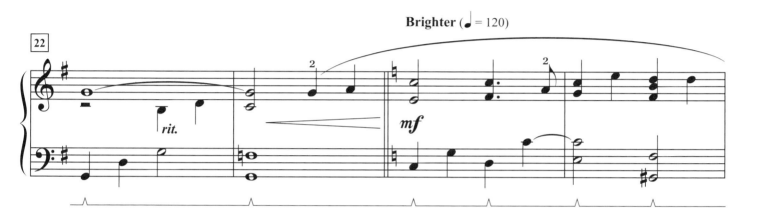

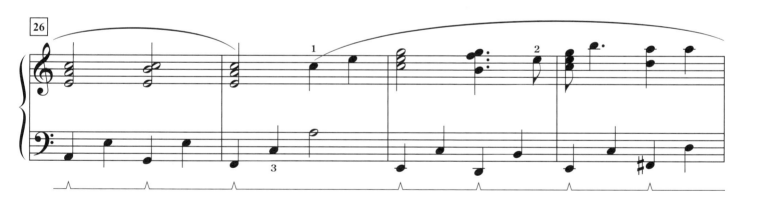

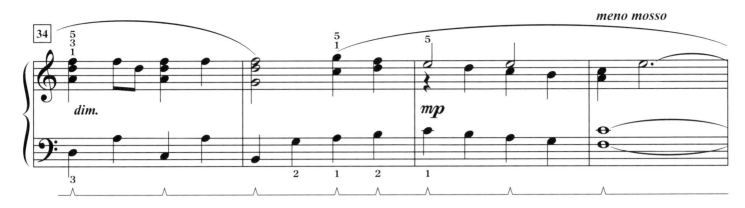

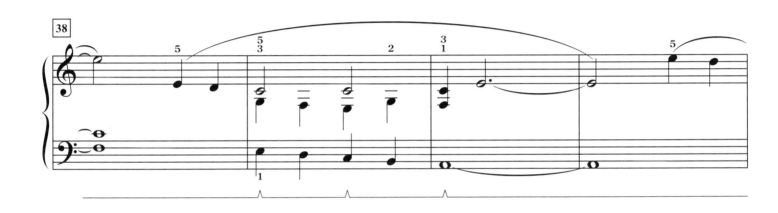

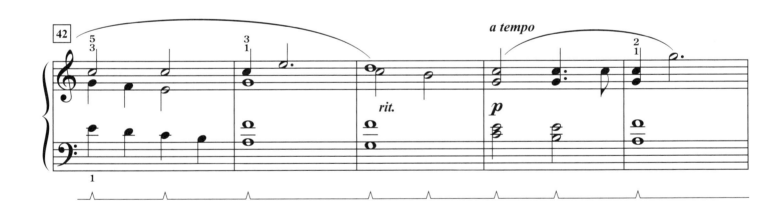

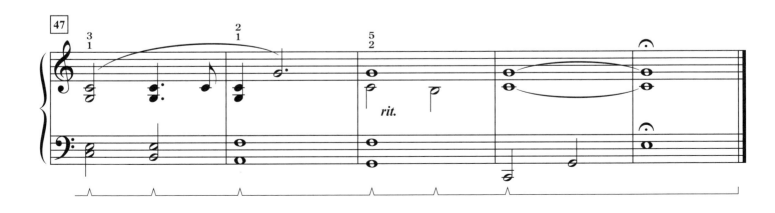

(Approx. Performance Time – 2:00)

O MIO BABBINO CARO

Giacomo Puccini
Arr. Victor Labenske

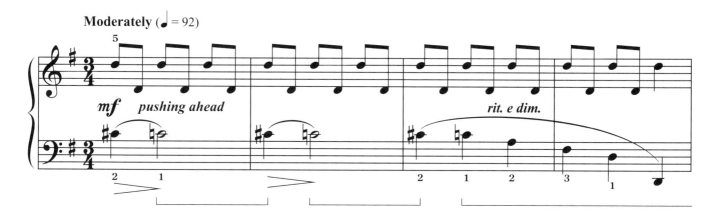

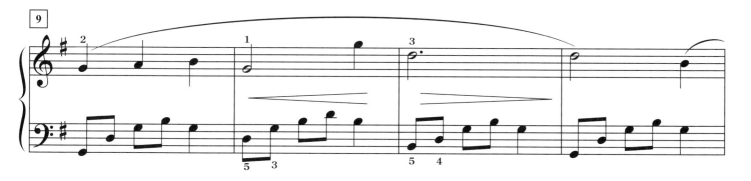

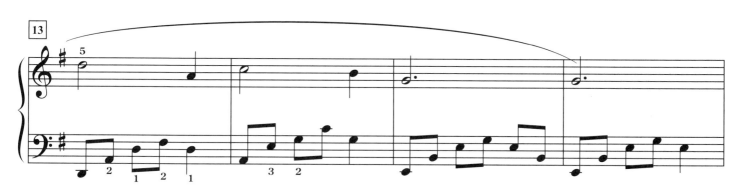

(Approx. Performance Time – 2:30)

O Happy Day

Anonymous, refrain attr. Edward F. Rimbault

Arr. Victor Labenske

(Approx. Performance Time – 2:30)

O Love That Will Not Let Me Go

In memory of my father, George Elbert Labenske

Albert L. Peace
Arr. Victor Labenske

(Approx. Performance Time – 2:00)

ON JORDAN'S STORMY BANKS

Traditional American Melody
Arr. Victor Labenske

With quiet anticipation (♩ = 63)

(Approx. Performance Time – 2:30)

Prince of Denmark's March

Jeremiah Clarke
Arr. Victor Labenske

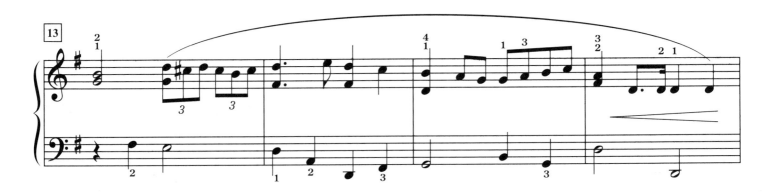

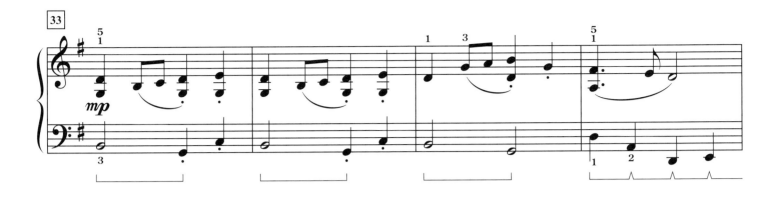

(Approx. Performance Time – 2:00)

SHALL WE GATHER AT THE RIVER

Robert Lowry
Arr. Victor Labenske

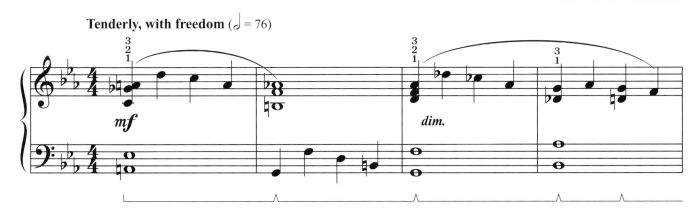

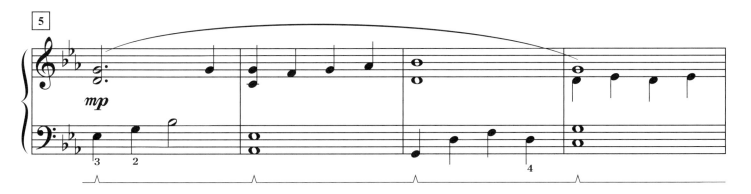

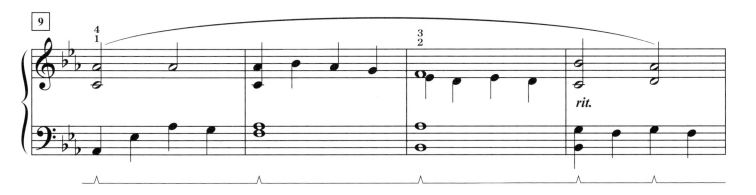

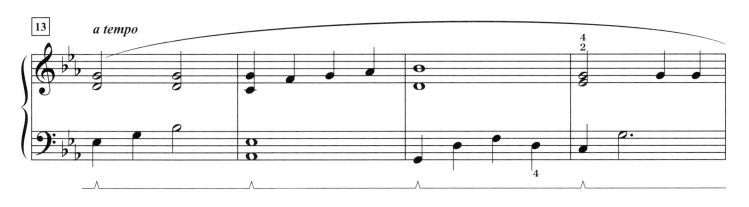

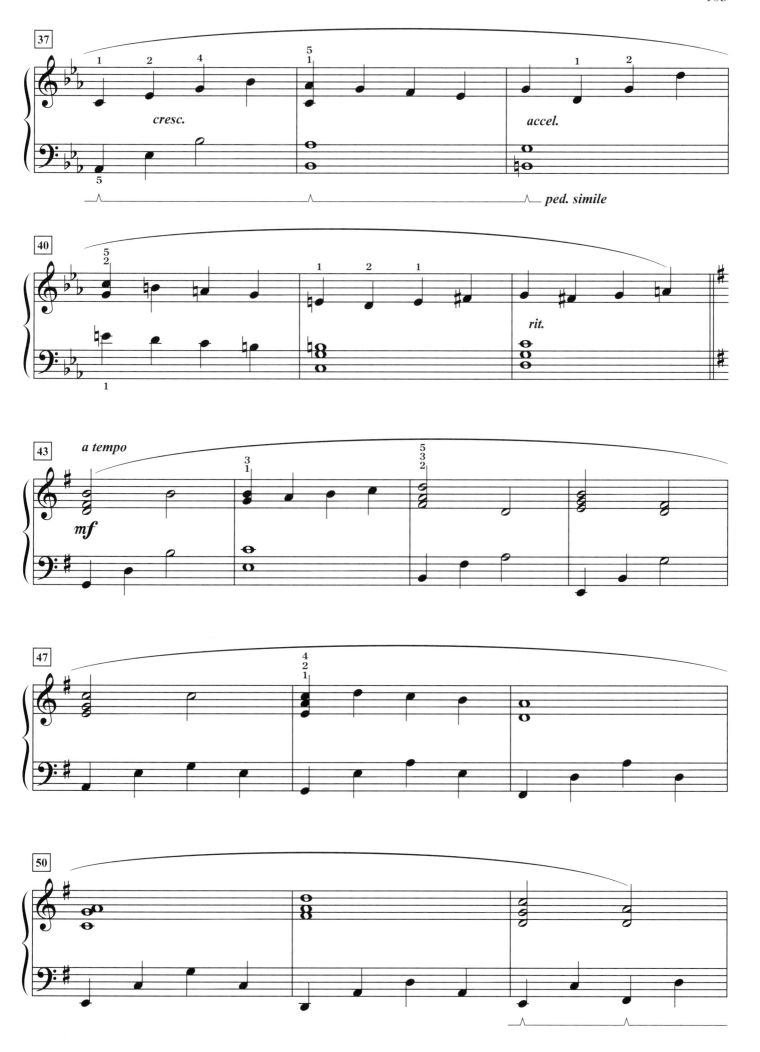

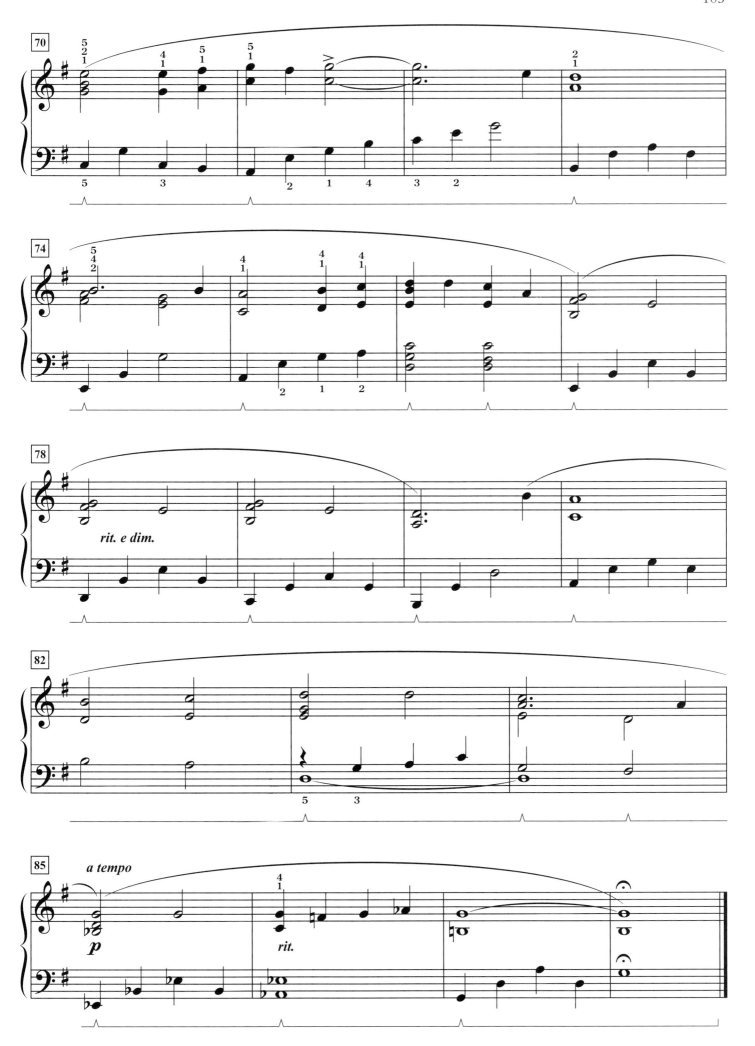

(Approx. Performance Time – 3:15)

ROCK OF AGES

Thomas Hastings
Arr. Victor Labenske

(Approx. Performance Time – 1:15)

TRUMPET TUNE

Henry Purcell
Arr. Victor Labenske

Note: For a shorter (16-measure) version, play A followed by C (skip B and D), or B followed by D (skip A and C).

Majestically (♩ = 100)

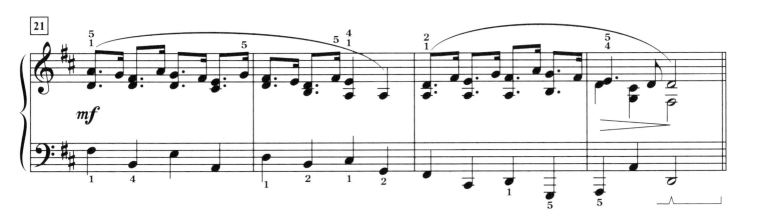

(Approx. Performance Time – 2:15)

THERE IS A BALM IN GILEAD

Spiritual
Arr. Victor Labenske

Soothingly ($\quarternote$ = 108)

(Approx. Performance Time – 2:15)

WE SHALL WALK THROUGH THE VALLEY IN PEACE

Spiritual
Arr. Victor Labenske

(Approx. Performance Time – 1:45)

WEDDING MARCH
FROM *A MIDSUMMER NIGHT'S DREAM*
(CONTEMPORARY VERSION)

Felix Mendelssohn
Arr. Victor Labenske

(Approx. Performance Time – 1:30)

WEDDING MARCH
FROM *A MIDSUMMER NIGHT'S DREAM*
(TRADITIONAL VERSION)

Felix Mendelssohn
Arr. Victor Labenske

(Approx. Performance Time – 2:45)

WHEN THE ROLL IS CALLED UP YONDER

James M. Black
Arr. Victor Labenske

128

(Approx. Performance Time – 0:30)

INCIDENTAL INTERLUDE NO. 1

Either of these pieces can be used for incidental music. For example, No. 1 might be played when the bride moves from the floor to the platform, and No. 2 might be played while the couple lights the unity candle.

Victor Labenske

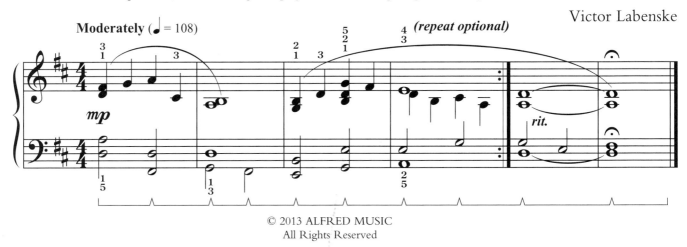

© 2013 ALFRED MUSIC
All Rights Reserved

(Approx. Performance Time – 1:00)

INCIDENTAL INTERLUDE NO. 2

Victor Labenske

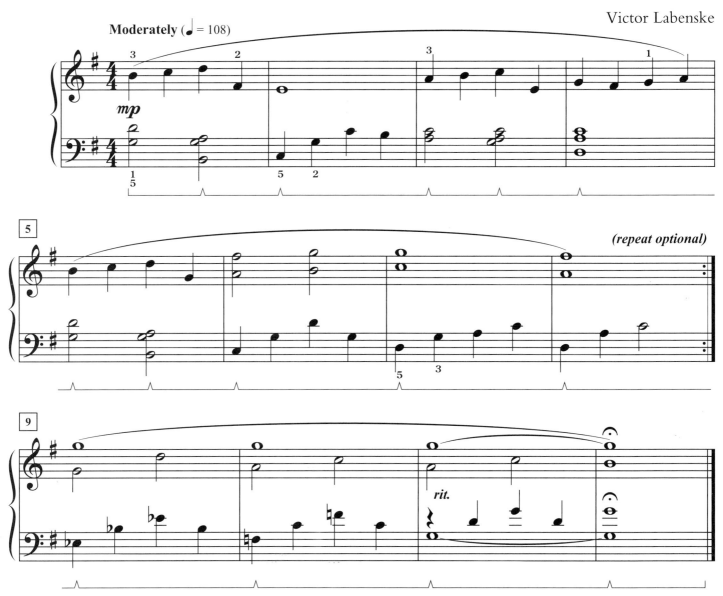

© 2013 ALFRED MUSIC
All Rights Reserved